STILL CHURCH?

CAN WE CONNECT DESPITE CORONA?

VAL FRASER

This book is dedicated to all those who lost their lives during the 2020 coronavirus pandemic.

May they rest in peace.

Published by inhousemedia

Copyright © Val Fraser 2020

The right of Val Fraser to be identified as the Author of the Work has been asserted by her in accordance with the Copyright, Designs and Patents Act 1988.

All rights reserved. No part of this publication may be reproduced, stored in a retrieval system, in any form or by any means whatsoever without the prior written permission of the publishers, nor be otherwise circulated in any form of binding or cover other than that in which it is published and without a similar condition being imposed on the subsequent purchaser. Brief quotations may be embedded in critical articles or reviews.

ISBN 978-0-9935749-8-6

Every reasonable effort has been made to trace copyright holders of material in this book, but if any have been inadvertently overlooked the publishers would be glad to hear from them and insert appropriate acknowledgements in any subsequent printing of this publication.

CONTENTS

1: ABSTENTION 9
2: AWARENESS 19
3: ALLIANCE 29
4: ALLEGIANCE 41
5: ALIGNMENT 53
6: ARCHITECTURE 65
7: ACCEPTANCE 77
8: ADAPTATIONS 89

INTRODUCTION

Our Father.

When Jesus was asked how we should pray 'Our' was the very first word he uttered.

Our.

Not I.

Not my.

Not their.

As someone who is responsible for crafting words I love the staggering genius and simplicity of this tactic. Many a writer carries the burden of knowing just how important their opening sentence, scene, phrase or word will be. For professional authors agonizing re-writes are not unusual. In the fast-paced world of news and media, readers can be lost within milliseconds if the headline and opening line doesn't have enough significance to hold their interest. This first word in the Lord's prayer communicates so much to me. It tells me, in just one word, that if I am going to pray Jesus recommends that I pray with others. It tells me that I wasn't designed to be alone, I was designed for fellowship with others.

There is power in this 'Our'.

And comfort.

And encouragement.

And belonging.

In spite of the coronavirus pandemic, subsequent social distancing and cancelled gatherings you are still part of this 'Our'. I like to think that the 'Our' which Jesus speaks of is a bond which cannot be broken by distance and space. The intrinsic connection can withstand a good deal of separation. The material in this book has been written to help you stay connected. It's not a bible study or devotional, it's a new kind of resource. I'm going to call it a 'connectional'.

I'm pretty sure that you won't find that word in the dictionary because I just made it up. Here's my definition:

> Connectional: (Noun) A digital or print resource which encourages regular discussion and prayer between two or more Christians during times of enforced social distancing, pestilence, plague or war.

It's perfectly feasible to work through this book by yourself. You may want to read the chapters, pray, journal and reflect upon the themes and questions in private. Or you may feel it would be helpful to use it as part of your weekly house group or bible study. Two close friends may be happy to share their thoughts by discussing the material over the phone. More than two people might wish to discuss the material via video call or pass their comments to each other via group email.

Whichever route you prefer it's my heartfelt prayer that, in spite of the current circumstances, you will grow and strengthen your sense of connection to other Christians.

Many members of the gathered church are dispersed. Freedom of movement is seriously limited. The normal activities of the church appear to be stilled. Wether we are enjoying this state of stillness or are thoroughly frustrated by it, I believe that we can still be the church.

Now more than ever the opening 'Our' of the Lord's prayer is vitally important. It stands eternal. When you are praying I would encourage you to think and pray in terms of 'our' and 'we' and 'us'. Join your prayers with the prayers of others.

The coronavirus pandemic may have limited our activities but the body of believers are **still church.**

Every blessing
Val Fraser

1: ABSTENTION

Britain is facing the unimaginable. The government has effectively forbidden Christians from meeting together. Surreal isn't it? But let's bear in mind that the government restriction is absolutely not based on religious grounds. And we are not on our own with this difficulty. Every gathering, for whatever reason, is deemed to be a risk. All groups of like-minded souls are facing the same social distancing. The restriction on gathering with others has been put into place to protect our health, our lives, and the health and lives of those we love. The decision makers in Britain are treating the risk of contracting and spreading coronavirus as a deadly serious threat. And so should we.

'Let us not give up meeting together . . .' Hebrews 10:25 NIV

These ancient words from the book of Hebrews encourage us to not give up meeting together, but for the time being we must give up meeting in large groups, as troubling as that is, we must. For the sake of those we love we must adhere to the guidelines. For those of us who are in the habit of gathering with other Christians, the current restrictions are a very difficult pill to swallow. Some of us may feel like children who are being administered with a foul tasting medicine, against our wishes, and being told "It's for our own good."

But let's pause here to consider for a moment the far less ancient, but helpful, metaphorical words of Mary Poppins. In the film of the same name she famously said: "A spoon full of sugar helps the medicine go down." The coronavirus pandemic is alarming, frightening even, absolutely for sure, but is it worth intentionally focusing on whatever sweetness we can find to offset our distress and discomfort?

In order to do that we will need to hold two opposite mind-sets in tension. Like two people travelling together in one car. From the passenger seat we hear the protective voice, anxious for our safety, which speaks of real worries. Real fear. Real concerns. Real changes. Real isolation. Real panic. Real loneliness. Real sickness. From the driver's seat we hear the protective voice which offers the sweetness of hope, new opportunities, longstanding truths, favourite verses, cherished hymns, current blessings, mature decisions, clear thinking, prayerful responses, God's faithfulness and the reminder that this too shall pass. There will always be two voices in the moving car of your mind. Always. Make friends with them both, be kind to them both, but be wise and vigilant about which one you allow to take the wheel.

So what silver linings might be found hiding within this particular cloud? Though none of us can gather in a group, thankfully we aren't forbidden from practising our faith. As individuals we can study, worship, pray and believe whatever we like. Precious freedom to practise one's chosen religion is still ours for the taking. We can choose to be inspired by favourite blogs, books and broadcasts. We can discover new sources of inspiration. We can encourage and pray over the phone with friends. If we are well enough we can go outdoors (while keeping our distance) and enjoy the beauty of God's creation. We can connect digitally. We can be intentional about blessing others. We can write letters.

The restrictions on meeting together give us a little better understanding of what it must be like for those who don't enjoy the same freedoms as we do. It brings new inspiration to pray and support them. We can be thankful for the many churches who have faithfully held public services for decades. Occasionally in recent years I've pondered the remote possibility that terrorism threats might close our doors. Or perhaps the powers behind political correctness might force us to shut the shop. But I never imagined for a moment that a tiny virus, invisible to the human eye, could bring about the involuntary abstention we are currently faced with.

Over the dark winter months I've been hunkered down capturing my thoughts and questions about church. As a perennially curious soul asking questions is present in both my DNA and my working life. I've been asking why do people go to church? What does church mean? How do others see it? How can we do it differently? I've wondered if the church didn't exist, would anyone miss it? Who would miss it? Why would they miss it? Now that many church buildings in Britain are temporarily closing for large gatherings, I'm feeling expectant that others may be urgently asking similar questions to mine. Out of this current chaos I pray that, along with a different way of being church, clear answers will emerge.

QUESTIONS FOR DISCUSSION AND REFLECTION

WHAT TROUBLES YOU THE MOST ABOUT THE CORONAVIRUS PANDEMIC?

WHAT WILL YOU MISS MOST ABOUT ATTENDING LIVE CHURCH GATHERINGS?

WHICH CANCELLED EVENTS, HOLIDAYS, APPOINTMENTS AND GATHERINGS ARE YOU MOST DISAPPOINTED ABOUT?

WHICH CANCELLATIONS ARE YOU FEELING RELIEVED ABOUT?

A prayer for protection

Heavenly Father please protect us, draw close to us during the daylight hours when we are faced with the troubling evaporation of normality.

Heavenly Father please calm us, draw close to us during the hours of darkness when the night thoughts loom large, give us peace and sound sleep.

Heavenly Father please comfort us, draw close to us when the grief of loss ambushes our souls, help us to accept the strange new landscape of our lives.

Heavenly Father please shield us and walk beside us when the firey darts of fear rain down from the high ground. Help us to be confident in you even in the valley of death.

Amen

Questions for Discussion and Reflection

In what ways are you intentionally taking responsibility for your health?

In what ways are you taking responsibility for your spiritual well-being?

Besides yourself, who do you feel a sense of responsibility towards?

Without putting yourself at risk is there someone you could keep an eye on?

A prayer for connectivity

Heavenly Father, thank you for our church community. During this strange season of social distancing please help us to be creative and intentional about maintaining and strengthening connections.

Heavenly Father thank you for the wonder of modern technology. During a time when many are self isolating please give us the courage to be bold and break new ground with digital technology.

Heavenly Father thank you for our friends and families. During a time when many are facing great uncertainty, perhaps losing their jobs and their identities, please help us to pray diligently and fervently for those we love and care about.

Heavenly Father thank you for the power of your Holy Spirit living within us, please help us to draw on that power. Remind us of all the things you have previously written on our hearts, give us the will to put them into practise.

Amen

2: AWARENESS

"Church is pointless."

When my teenage son declared this damning indictment he was implementing the use of the word 'church' in only one of its many meanings. In the UK the word 'church' is commonly used interchangeably to mean several things. So when he posed the question "What's the Point of Church?" in reality, it was more like asking several questions all rolled into one. Upon hearing that question, each listener will have a different understanding of the question, depending upon which meaning of the word 'church' they are 'hearing'. Already, you may have made up your own mind what that question ought to mean and what the answer ought to be. But your 'oughts' are likely to be very different to the 'oughts' of another person. How then might it be possible for me to gather consistent answers to a question which is fundamentally inconsistent in meaning?

When my teenage son voiced his rather rude statement regarding church, I was immediately able to make the following interpretation: In that instance I understood that the word 'church' meant the specific experience of a Sunday morning meeting. So often when the word church is used, especially by church-goers, what they're often referring to is that specific 60-120 minute window of time when the 'church members' meet up, often on a Sunday morning as in the statement "I'm going to church".

It's my observation that for some people, activities and meetings which fall outside of this window aren't commonly referred to as 'church'. That isn't necessarily an accurate reflection on the opinion of the speaker. It may not mean they believe these activities are not 'church'. They may well place enormous value on weekday activities but for purposes of clarity they just can't use that word to describe it. The word church already has multiple meanings. It's stretched about as far as it can be stretched. It cannot reasonably be expected to encompass even one more use without becoming so nuanced that it loses its meaning altogether.

"The church is beautiful." When my friend made this statement during her attendance at a traditional candle lit Christmas service she was implementing one of the most common uses of the word 'church'. We can easily interpret her meaning. Of course she was referring to the building. Even today, a traditional church building can command considerable admiration from visitors. When the coronavirus pandemic began to unfold I came across the following statement on social media: "I see the churches are shutting down". I understand that in this case, the comment was referring to a physical building where church members meet regularly.

"The church is growing." When a church leader makes this statement in the Annual Report he isn't referring to the size of the building or the expanding amount of time the Sunday morning meeting will occupy. In all likelihood he is using the word 'church' as it was originally used, as a collective verb to describe the numbers of living, flesh and blood believers. To further confuse matters I've also heard this term used in reference to spiritual growth. So while it can mean there are more new members, it may also mean there actually aren't any new members, but the current ones have grown spiritually 'bigger'.

"The church is dying." When you come across a media headline such as this you may quickly come to understand that it isn't making reference to either a single Sunday morning meeting or a single church building. In almost all circumstances this kind of use constitutes the much broader reference which relates to a large church organisation. It may be a local, national or even global denominational structure. It may be a group of churches. It may even be a vague reference to every church denomination and every church everywhere, amalgamated into one convenient lump!

Sometimes we use the word church to describe just a single meaning, sometimes two, three or even all of them. The potential for confusion, both inside and outside the church organisation, is very real. But the meanings do matter. When my teenage son said that "church was pointless" we talked further and I discovered that my initial guess was correct. He really hadn't enjoyed the experience of attending the meeting and wanted to express that as strongly as he dared to. He wasn't referring to the building, the broader organisation of the church, my church friends or even his own friends. He'd just had a difficult morning and needed to be honest about that.

QUESTIONS FOR DISCUSSION AND REFLECTION

NAME SOME OF THE DIFFERENT WAYS YOU USE THE WORD CHURCH. HOW MANY CAN YOU THINK OF?

DO YOU THINK THE WAY WE USE WORDS AND LANGUAGE CHANGES OVER THE COURSE OF TIME?

HOW HAS THE ESTABLISHED CHURCH CHANGED IN YOUR LIFETIME?

HOW DO YOU FEEL ABOUT THESE CHANGES?

A prayer about words

Heavenly Father, thank you for giving us the gift of words and language. Help us to to overlook and stay silent about the flaws and weaknesses we might perceive in others and instead use our words wisely, to bless and encourage them.

Heavenly Father, during these turbulent times help us to find our place and purpose within the community of faith as it currently exists. Dispel the fearful whispering voices which may tell us that church has become pointless and that it will never recover from the coronavirus pandemic.

Heavenly Father, help us to graciously accept the uncomfortable limitations placed upon us. Help us to graciously accept the assistance we may need from others. Help us to graciously accept your unchanging love and demonstrable favour.

Amen

QUESTIONS FOR DISCUSSION AND REFLECTION

WHAT IMPACT HAS THE CORONAVIRUS PANDEMIC HAD ON YOUR SPIRITUAL LIFE?

WHAT IMPORTANT PLANS AND HOPES ARE YOU HAVING TO LET GO OF?

CAN YOU RECALL A TIME WHEN GOD BROUGHT YOU THROUGH A PARTICULARLY DARK VALLEY?

A prayer for help

Heavenly Father, help us to remember that we are your church, we are one body, remind us that we are not alone and we have brothers and sisters in Christ who are also coping in difficult circumstance. Help us to find new ways to connect with others in the body.

Heavenly Father, as we grieve for the future we believed we would have, help us to let go of all the hopes and plans we had and release all that we are and have into your hands. Help us to trust you.

Heavenly Father, by the power of your Holy Spirit reveal to us your hand at work in our lives during the last twelve months. Show us the blessings which you have already put into place to prepare us for such a time as this. Open our eyes to see your far sighted love in action.

Heavenly Father, by the power of your Holy Spirit reveal to us new ways of being church, new and creative ways of connecting with others, new and creative ways of structuring our days and weeks around you.

Amen

3: ALLIANCE

If you head west out of the English Lake District town of Coniston, and follow the pleasant narrow path along a disused railway line, you'll soon find yourself in deepest sheep country. When the path ends, and the ground rises over the line, follow the gentle bend in the road. Climb over the stile into the rolling meadow and there, behind the shelter of a substantial dry stone boundary wall, you'll happen upon a rather handsome stone bench. And here I must register my grateful thanks towards the masterful hand which crafted it and their entirely genius decision to place it precisely where it is. From this wonderful vantage point, it's possible to rest one's weary laurels and enjoy magnificent panoramic views of the sweeping valley dramatically framed by the mountains beyond. It's a moment of glorious natural theatre. A quiet perch, a flask of tea and a cracking view were now mine for the taking.

The pastoral scene was idyllic. Dotted around each patchwork field were grazing sheep and their lambs. I watched for some time as, just a few yards away, the cutest pair of twins waggled their little tails while feeding stop-start from their patiently waiting Mum. All this new life awakened a little broodiness. The wholesome maternal setting, generated a warm glow within me and I relaxed into the kind embrace of Mother Earth.

BAA-AAAA! BAA-AAA!

My lovely mood was sharply interrupted by an intense wave of panic, as out of nowhere, a sort of sheep riot broke out. All at once the ewes kicked off, excitedly BAA-BAA-ing at high volume. Suddenly animated and awakened from their zombie-like state, a hundred noisy sheep began stampeding towards me. Or where they aiming for the gate nearby? As the pack approached me the sheep quickly grew from fluffy white dots set quaintly against the mossy earth, into scarily large animals each one about the size of a 2009 Volvo Estate. And they were moving just as fast. Even the lambs now appeared to be as big as the very biggest of freakishly big dogs.

Momentarily that troubling scene from the blockbuster movie Jurassic Park played out in my mind's eye. Y'know, the one where the man-eating dinosaurs begin hunting the main characters? I hear that low voice whisper cautiously into my ear: "They're learning." Then Dr Alan Grant played by the actor Sam Neill issues his final steely warning: "RUN!" And seriously, when Sam Neill tells you to run, you know you that it is indeed time to run.

Thoroughly intimidated by this rowdy baying gang I immediately began mentally calibrating the fastest escape route out of the field. Would I make it back over the stile before they reached me or should I take my chances clambering over the rugged dry stone wall behind me? Should I drop the flask of tea and run? Could I successfully scramble up a bony fleece strewn wall while clutching a kit kat in one hand? Could I devour the kit kat before they crushed me under their horrible pointy cloven hooves? Should I sacrifice my kit kat to this marauding mob? And an important existential question I ask myself on most days of the week - should I value my continued survival more than I value my tea and my kit kat? Hmmmm. So many questions. So many, many, tough choices.

My nerves were sheep wrecked. But my alarm subsided when I realised that the shepherd was at work in a neighbouring field. He was dumping a load of extra feed for another flock. It appeared to be this activity which had aroused them from their gentle grazing. His voice had plunged them all into a brief period of concerted action before they dissipated harmlessly and went back to the everyday business of nibbling the ground. By the end of my exhausting, in depth sheep research, an observation period lasting the length of an average tea break, it became apparent to me that sheep aren't the brightest. They're not at all organised. I remain unconvinced they can even communicate with each other. When one sheep starts walking in a particular direction the rest aimlessly follow.

As far as I could tell the sheep in this field seemed to be a disparate group of individuals, disorganised, totally lacking in collaboration, without team spirit, cohesion, leadership, strategy, rank or hierarchical structure. How can they be so short sighted that they just do their business and eat on the same piece of ground? How bad is that? Obviously I'm not the first person on the planet to make this alarming discovery, but it was bombshell news to me.

Neither, I happily concede, am I the first person to make religious comparisons or draw spiritual conclusions from the universally understood imagery of sheep and shepherds. Is the sheep metaphor is half-baked insult or a term of endearment? Was Jesus being kind or comical? Does the divine consider us to be equally loveable members of a dozy species, equally vulnerable, equally short-sighted, equally disorganised, largely disconnected from our fellow sheep, heads down, fully consumed by the day to day tasks of survival, sleep walking through the field of life, wandering directionless in among our own mess?

Right up until the 'riot' incident, observing the sheep grazing was largely a peaceful, uneventful activity. I still can't make up my mind if sheep are blissfully contented creatures, happy with their lot in life, or aimless, inactive spongers. Are they humbly accepting their allocated circumstances or are they making the absolute least possible effort to get by? Are they wise and confident with a firm understanding of their station in life, knowing who they are and where they fit into the bigger picture of the natural order? Or are they totally lacking in drive and ambition and any desire to make even the tiniest of improvements to their existence?

There's lots that I just don't know about sheep. So I'll tell you what I do know. When those fluffy headed critters heard the shepherd's voice from the other side of the hill, and they sensed he was near, I saw it for myself, they were immediately transformed into creatures of considerable purpose and direction.

Without hesitation they filled the valley with the strangely human, deep yearning chorus of their voices. With growing momentum they seemed to become of one mind, somehow drawn together in a woolly exodus, each one gathered up from the far corners of this patch of earth. They appeared out of the shade, casting lumpy shadows in the sunshine. They tumbled out of the sheltered areas and trotted merrily into the open spaces. They emerged from in among the shrubs and from the cosy bases of the dry stone walls around the perimeter. They were uprooted from their sitting and awakened from their sleeping.

They were organically united and moved across the pasture like a wave breaking onto the shore in one precise, clear geometrically accurate direction. They lifted their heads from the grubby earth. They looked up. They called out in a rising crescendo of deep throaty bleats. They strode purposefully, eagerly moving towards the place where they could hear the shepherd's voice, where they knew he was at work. Just out of sight. Beyond the wooden criss-cross gate. Over the bosom of the hill. Suddenly they all seemed to be part of a powerful military alliance. The transformation was really quite remarkable.

And surely this scene offers us a visual representation of an astonishing claim. One of the most outrageous messages of Christianity posits that when people are united by the words of Jesus, a group of individuals can suddenly become a force to be reckoned with. The powerful potential of 'group think' is awakened. The potential to move in the same direction. To become organised into a group which is no longer a collection of individuals focused purely on their own self-interests, but a collective, working together for the good of others. They become greater than the sum of their parts.

Long ago there was a word which was used to describe this alliance, this behaving as a group or team in response to the words of Jesus. When this happened, when people voluntarily gathered together to form a platoon with a purpose, however big or small, the name they were given was the 'church'. Long before there were buildings and places of Christian worship, long before the people had a place to meet or an ornate three tier pulpit carved from oak, before the Christian faith was hijacked by the rich and powerful, the people and the actions surrounding them, were simply known as the 'church'.

QUESTIONS FOR DISCUSSION AND REFLECTION

HAVE YOU SEEN THE FILM JURASSIC PARK? DID YOU ENJOY IT?

DO YOU THINK SHEEP AND SHEPHERDS ARE AN ACCURATE REPRESENTATION OF CHRIST AND CHRISTIANS?

CAN YOU RECALL SOMETHING WHICH LEFT YOU FEELING EMBARRASSED TO BE A CHRISTIAN?

CAN YOU RECALL SOMETHING WHICH LEFT YOU FEELING PROUD TO BE A CHRISTIAN?

A prayer of thanks

Heavenly Father, thank you that your word includes stories with helpful rural and farming imagery which we can see and understand for ourselves today. Help us, where possible, to access open places and fresh air, and speak to us through the beauty of your creation.

Heavenly Father, Loving Father, help us to accept the kindness of your guiding hand at work in our lives and our land.

Heavenly Father, when we are feeling shut in or are experiencing the personal cave of self isolation, give us the same resolve as your servant, King David. When we are surrounded by an invisible enemy, help us, like David, to be intentional about remembering your past goodness towards us and to sing your praises even in the darkness.

Heavenly Father, thank you for the gift of living things to love and care for - our pets, our house plants and gardens. In these difficult times help us to take our eyes off the storm, to limit our consumption of news, to pause and marvel at the wonder of life.
Amen

QUESTIONS FOR DISCUSSION AND REFLECTION

DO YOU HAVE UNDERLYING HEALTH CONDITIONS? ARE YOU IN THE VULNERABLE CATEGORY?

HOW DO YOU FEEL YOUR HEALTH 'STATUS' AFFECTS YOUR PERSONAL IDENTITY?

HOW DO YOU TYPICALLY RESPOND TO FEARFUL THOUGHTS, ABOUT YOUR OWN HEALTH AND THE HEALTH OF OTHERS?

WHAT POSITIVE LEGACY COULD THE PANDEMIC CRISIS LEAVE?

Prayers

Heavenly Father, in some tangible way, please remind us just how much you value and love the broken things of this world. Remind us that you don't measure us the way human eyes might, please allow us to catch a glimpse of your loving care for us.

Heavenly Father, please meet us in our moments of fear and isolation, give us strategies to shunt out our own negativity or thoughtless comments which might come against us, leaving us troubled. Spare us from fretting and ruminating about what might go wrong next. Help us to focus on the good which may come out of this situation and give us bright hope in these dark times.

Heavenly Father, please walk closely alongside us when we are well and when we are unwell. Stay so close Father. Help us to confidently declare your goodness towards us.

Heavenly Father, please be with those who must carry on with their jobs. Protect the delivery drivers, the NHS staff, the emergency services, the care workers and those who supply us with food. Help us to support them in prayer and by all means possible.

Amen

4: ALLEGIANCE

Strains of *Sweet Chariot* grow ever louder. The rain hammers down without mercy. The Guinness flows. A beautiful kick by Farrell. The crowd bounces with gleeful cheer. Tensions rise. Excitement mounts. We're close to the end. The seconds are ticking. I watch, unaware that within a few days the coronavirus pandemic will shut down the whole shooting match. The Six Nations Rugby Championship is well underway and the Scottish team are going head to head with the English team.

But to which players have I pledged my allegiance? Exactly where does my loyalty and commitment lie? Who am I cheering for?

Turns out I'm cheering for anyone who's doing their level best. I'm even cheering for the referee because he seems like a decent bloke. The camera and production crews are doing a sterling job. The commentators are on top form. So whose side am I actually on? I can claim genuine Scottish, English and Irish ancestry. This is one of the very few matches where I just can't lose. My somewhat fickle allegiance will, for the remainder of the weekend at least, rest firmly with the winning side, whoever they are. By the end of today I will be victorious. It's a certainty. I will happily identify with whichever team wins the match. "A filthy, ugly game" the commentator spits out with a bright resounding Celtic force. In this battle only one team will be the conquerors. And it will be my team. My boys will win. And after downing a couple of Guinness, that seems like a perfectly fair and reasonable outcome to me.

And isn't that the way? Honestly? Don't we naturally prefer to identify with the winning team? And, depending on how poorly they've played, we might want to distance ourselves from the losing team. Unpacking this, in terms of any kind of allegiance we may have towards a faith organisation, is a complex matter. If a particular denomination or church leader is on the receiving end of bad press the shock waves reach far beyond their immediate circle. The whole organisation can quickly fall into disrepute. Faithful supporters may feel badly let down and may voice their disillusionment.

They may withdraw their giving. Those in positions of power or influence are often quick to make public statements about their take on the matter. Sometimes these statements are supportive, at other times they denounce any connection to the leader in question. The public pile in; adding fuel to the fire. It's a different kind of "filthy, ugly game" but the 'managers' are still the ones in the firing line. In faith organisations the winners and losers aren't nearly as clear cut as they are in sporting events. And some players may be so desperately wounded and damaged that they never find the strength to return to the arena. Not even as a spectator.

Dare I make reference to political parties at this juncture? The never ending game of politics, both at home and abroad seems to have grown especially "filthy and ugly" to me of late. I'm currently disinclined to pledge my allegiance to anyone at national level. Perhaps I'm being naïve. I'm definitely shirking my civic duty. I feel pretty lousy about that actually, especially in view of all those women who campaigned and sacrificed so that I could vote. For two months I stopped watching the news on television. The first couple of weeks were so liberating that it took a while for me to resume the habit. I've been less inclined to engage with political stories than I've ever been. In some respects I stand in awe of working politicians because of their tenacity to stay in such a brutal game. They face such cruel public scrutiny. It's a marvel that they manage to win the allegiance of a single constituent, let alone turn up for work and do their actual job. Before the coronavirus pandemic filled the news I noticed myself dodging stories about politics whenever they popped up on social media too. My mood improved but the guilt crushed me.

Perhaps to some extent this need we feel to be counted with the winning team is rooted in how we perceive what perception others have of us. I'll say that again. Our allegiance may be influenced by how we perceive *others are perceiving us because of the team, tribe or group to which we belong.* Figuratively speaking each of us loosely belongs to a poorly defined tribe, by birth or by choice. Human beings are tribal by nature. This makes it all too easy to be judged as guilty, or not guilty, by association. Such perceptions can and do affect our acceptance and inclusion by others in broader society.

Our perceived 'tribal membership' can, for instance, affect whether or not our children get a place in the local primary school, whether we're offered a job, whether we're invited to the networking party. The Oxford Graduate is more likely to secure the high level job than the ex-con. The ex-con is more likely to be invited to join the local mafia than the Oxford Grad. The well connected London based journalist with a 'Fleet Street' pedigree is more likely to secure the lucrative publishing deal than the unknown working class northerner beavering away out in the back of beyond (not that I'm bitter). These perceptions about which tribe we are notionally part of, ill-defined and illusive as they are, matter quite a lot.

Did you, as a teenager or young adult, ever feel embarrassed by your parents or relatives? Were you embarrassed by the area you lived in or the school you attended? Perhaps you weren't posh enough.

Perhaps you were too posh. Of course you eventually grew out of this extreme self-consciousness which is so characteristic of adolescence. Did you? Maybe not entirely. Being a person of faith is a rewarding path which many folks choose, but it also opens up a whole world of competing loyalties, commitments and potential embarrassments.

To whom have you pledged your allegiance? The trendy burgeoning mega-church may seem like the cool place to be, but does the celebritization of its leaders make you feel uncomfortable? The concert type worship may be exhilarating but does the hyped up sermon exhorting you to be a 'totally awesome dude' leave you feeling exhausted? The traditional church may seem stable and accountable, but does the glacial pace of change paralyse your hopes for improvement? The richness of ancient liturgy may stir your soul but does the stand-up-sit-down routine jangle your nerves? The warmth of maternal fellowship may be deeply comforting but does belonging to an old dear's club undermine your hard earned street cred?

The very act of choosing to pledge allegiance and self-identify yourself with any group of humans, anywhere on the planet, has the inherent potential to cause you irritation, embarrassment, and even shame, as sure as day follows night. It's an inescapable part of our flawed humanity. No sports team, no political party, no faith group, no church community, no educational institution, no geographical area, no wider family, no profession, no collection of living, breathing human beings are exempt from making mistakes and getting it wrong, sometimes terribly wrong. Fellow members of your chosen 'tribe' may even offend you. They may go off in a different direction than originally promised or expected. Leaders in particular, and their associated agendas, may come and then quite unexpectedly go.

We may crave stability but to expect it all the time is certain folly. Expectations of non-stop perfect conditions for personal comfort and fulfilment may seem hopeful but they aren't rooted in reality. If we pledge our allegiance, that is to say our loyalty and commitment, to a group of fellow humans we must keep our expectations at a realistic level, or face up to the eventual disappointment. There is no ideal tribe. People can, and most likely will, let us down. But we in turn can certainly, by design or default, let others down. When we have learned to live, and indeed thrive, under the almost unbearable of weight of this truth we can be free from the superficial and often fickle allegiances of tribe. The value of this freedom can't be understated.

I say fickle because it's all too easy, in our flawed humanity, to transfer our favour to the winning team. For all the world it appeared as though I was switching sides during the Six Nations Rugby Championship. But in my heart, in the very deepest part of me, I was delighting in the human endeavour on display. I was proud of the skill, the effort, the split second decisions, the honour, the fairness, the justice. When my children were younger they sometimes protested "You're always on his side!" My answer was always the same. "I'm the Mum. I'm on everyone's side." It can be a little disarming when we consider that God may be on everyone's side. Perhaps He too sits on the side-lines, simply delighting in the effort of our human endeavour. Perhaps God doesn't even see 'sides' in the way we do. Perhaps, in the face of much social and economic turbulence, fairness and kindness and love are the things which register with Him.

QUESTIONS FOR DISCUSSION AND REFLECTION

IF YOU'VE EVER ATTENDED OR WATCHED A MAJOR SPORTING EVENT HOW WAS THAT EXPERIENCE FOR YOU?

WHICH INDIVIDUALS DO YOU FEEL LOYALTY TOWARDS?

WHICH WIDER ORGANISATIONS DO YOU FEEL LOYALTY TOWARDS?

DO YOU HAVE A FAVOURITE CHARITY OR CAUSE WHICH YOU ARE HELPING (OR WISH YOU COULD HELP)?

Prayers

Heavenly Father, you know the true allegiances of our hearts, test us and know our anxious thoughts and lead us in your ways.

Heavenly Father, in these uncertain times when everything is being shaken, help us to let go of any human allegiances or affections which are stronger than our allegiance and our affections towards you. And forgive us our weakness in pinning our hopes on such temporal things.

Heavenly Father, in these troubling times, help us to forgo seeking the shallow fleeting comforts which the world offers, but to seek and receive our deep and lasting comfort and security directly from knowing you. And forgive us our weakness in chasing after worldly pleasures.

Heavenly Father, in these challenging times let us not be found wanting. Help us, by the power of your Holy Spirit to make wise choices, to study your word, to read inspirational books, to listen to inspirational worship and teachings.

Amen

QUESTIONS FOR DISCUSSION AND REFLECTION

WHAT'S THE BIGGEST GROUP OF PEOPLE YOU HAVE EVER WORSHIPPED WITH?

HAVE YOU EVER WORSHIPPED ALONE?

WHEN WAS THE LAST TIME YOU FELT GOD SPEAK TO YOU? WHAT DID HE SAY?

DO YOU KEEP A JOURNAL OF YOUR PRAYER AND SPIRITUAL LIFE?

Prayers

Heavenly Father, during this time of social distancing help us to draw closer to you than ever before, help us to believe and claim the promise that you in turn will draw close to us.

Heavenly Father, as we separate ourselves from our usual gatherings, help us to remember that your allegiance lies firmly with us. That you hold us in your hand. That you never let us go, even when we drift away. No scheme of man can ever take us from your hand.

Heavenly Father, though we are weak and fickle you love us still, bind up our wounds, grant us health, shore up our immune systems, help us to be diligent with social distancing.

Heavenly Father, we are in this for the long haul, grant us patience with ourselves and with others, thank you for this opportunity to develop strong spiritual endurance and resilience, Lord keep cheering us on as we aim higher!

Amen

5. ALIGNMENT

"I'm up for this challenge, I want to do it, but not with them, please not them!"

Working in collaboration with others has to be one of the most testing, trying, troubling, tricky, treacherous endeavours one human being can possibly get involved with. Surely it's far less risky and complicated to work with babies, children, cats, dogs, panthers, snakes, zombies, lions, tigers and bears than with our fellow adults. What with all their opinions and agendas and messiness.

Before the social distancing which the coronavirus pandemic brought into force the prospect of working alongside difficult others could make the idea of prolonged isolation seem quite attractive. Retreating into our own corners will be a new experience for many. The benefits and battles of solitude may concentrate our minds and perhaps we will emerge from the siege softer, stronger, more tolerant. More ready to engage, to marvel at the complex wonder of human company, conversation and collaboration.

The challenge of working with others can be especially difficult for the more relational types among us. If we crave uninterrupted harmony, peace and friendship, working with others can be the most almighty shock to the system. What if we don't agree? What if our values are different? What if their opinions differ to ours? What if there's conflict? What if we aren't aligned in our vision and purpose? Yikes! How awkward is that going be?

We can get into a right old tangle when working with others. Sometimes our personal viewpoints and attitudes can unknowingly contribute to the complexity. We may have excitedly joined a team, or taken on a new job in a new setting. When we were looking in from the outside everything looked perfectly fine. But as our close encounters with colleagues rack up it's a shock if we discover discord between team members. It's a crushing disappointment when we believe we've landed our dream role, only to discover that the vision and purpose of key members of the organisation are not fully aligned. When the reality of this misalignment finally dawns on us, we can feel tricked and angry.

Media and publishing can be a fast-paced, brutal, dog-eat-dog sort of world. So you may not be surprised to learn that I've found myself feeling suitably 'tricked' on more than one occasion. You wouldn't be on your own if you're the sort of person who believes these situations are a 'test' from God. Some very spiritual folks firmly believe this to be the case. I've heard it stated that if you fail the test, you get to do a re-sit. Again. And again. Until you pass.

I'm not a trained theologian so I feel utterly ill-equipped to offer any valuable insight into whether God is the originator of such tests. But I do know that difficult scenarios have a way of returning to haunt us. It can seem as if we're facing exactly the same problem again further down the line. Is this because we have a personal weakness or failing? Perhaps it's because we're all flawed and immature and some of the difficulties we face when dealing with others are just part of the process of normal human development. Working with others shapes us, hopefully for the better. It gives us the conditions in which to grow. In wise company we can become more mature and tolerant towards those who don't share our opinions.

When vision and purpose within a team have been fully aligned I've found that to be among the most rewarding and productive periods of my life. Truly. It's a kind of magic. Team members brought out the best in each other. Ideas were bounced around. There was mutual respect. There was much laughter. There was the deep satisfaction of meaningful hard graft. At the end of the project there was a pint in the pub and the relaxed elation of a successful team effort. It was the best of times.

When vision and purpose within a team have not been aligned I've found that to be among the least rewarding and productive periods of my life. It was the pits. A relational hell. Team members brought out the worst in each other. Ideas were surreptitiously stolen. There was zero mutual respect. There was gossip. There was the deep dissatisfaction of meaningless hard graft. At the end of the project there was a pint in the pub and outright competitiveness about who would claim the credit for it. It was the worst of times.

In the bright fertile environment of fully aligned thinking my creativity and enthusiasm have thrived and blossomed. In the barren environment of bitter misalignment my creativity and enthusiasm have withered on the vine. Turns out I wasn't very nice when my creativity and enthusiasm withered. Turns out that when someone I trusted had stolen my ideas I was a cow. When my livelihood was threatened I wasn't at all gracious. When colleagues traded snippets of potentially advantageous tittle tattle I played the game too. When hard graft became meaningless I was grumpy. When unscrupulous colleagues in the pub received the credit for my ingenious creative ideas I morphed into a witchy prideful snob stirring toothless curses into my beer. I failed the blinking test. I totally bombed.

It took some time to let go of the shame I experienced from failing my tests. I could have behaved better and God knows I am dreadfully sorry for that. But here's the thing, while the alignment of thinking about vision and purpose might just naturally emerge within a team, it might not. And that's why we need strong leadership. Without leadership the ship is rudderless and bedlam breaks out. And that's bad. When there's turbulence at leadership level, especially in a paid work situation where livelihoods are at stake, team members begin pushing and shoving to take control. It's 'every man for himself'. Insecurity prevails. Threat detection systems are launched. Panic ensues. No one knows where they fit in anymore and the whole structure of the previously accepted dominance hierarchy comes crashing down.

Alignment of vision and purpose lives in the same neighbourhood as something which faith based organisations often refer to as 'unity'. When teams are willing to get behind a strong leader and work together in unity they can bring about great good, far more good than they could ever achieve working independently. When unity is absent in communities, work places and even nations, they will naturally achieve less. When there is active dis-unity and discord in communities, work places and nations, members can expend all their energies on tearing each other apart. It takes a massive peace keeping exercise just to restore harmony.

To my great astonishment there are those among us, alive and walking this very planet as we speak, who are seriously gifted in the fearful art of peace making. They do not shy away from untangling difficulties. They're drawn to it. They thrive on it. They bring order out of chaos. It's a wonderful thing to behold. Actually quite beautiful in its own way. The courage of these folks staggers me, it honestly does.

I've survived enough raw conflict to last seven life times and would run a Cornish mile before signing up for more. But the gifted peace maker doesn't seem to fear human discord. Rather they're called to place themselves right in the epicentre of the storm. They allow themselves to be the buffer between angry opponents. They absorb the negative energy and transpose it into light. The peace makers roll up their sleeves and get stuck into the risky, unpredictable, potentially dangerous excavation work of relational war. They deconstruct and dispose of ramshackle and out-dated arguments. They clear away anything which obstructs alignment of vision and purpose. They prepare the way for those who will do the messy, back breaking groundwork of productive future alliances.

As the coronavirus epidemic unfolds everyone is facing a very different future to the one they were hoping for. Churches, schools, pubs, cinemas, cafes and restaurants have closed for business. All my plans for the year have evaporated. I have deleted every gig and gathering from my diary. I'm not sure when I'll see the people I love. This is painful and difficult to deal with. There is much uncertainty. I'm just one person, what can I do in the face of such a mighty enemy? I've decided to pray for unity and alignment among leaders of every religious and political hue. I shall follow the guidelines and pray for those who are facing the challenges of making difficult decisions which affect all of us. I shall believe and hope that as we stand together against this deadly common foe it will generate enough healthy fear to vanquish petty squabbling. I shall pray that as leaders and commoners alike pour their energies into the crucible of creative problem solving God himself will burn off differences and bring us all into alignment with each other, really and truly I will.

Questions for Discussion and Reflection

Have you ever worked on a project in collaboration with others?

Have you ever worked on a project in total isolation?

Which leaders do you most admire and why?

Are leaders or individuals responsible for the direction of the church? How do you see it?

Prayers

Heavenly Father, we are sorry for the times when we have been difficult to work with, when our own need for recognition has got in the way, when we have needed to be right, when we have been the source of distress for others.

Heavenly Father, we are sorry for our unwillingness to let others take the credit for our efforts, we are sorry for our human frailty, for our sins against you and our fellow man.

Heavenly Father, during this time of great distress and worry for many people, through the power of your Holy Spirit, help us to be part of the solution and not part of the problem, give us the grace to be the peacemakers, the comforters, the encouragers.

Heavenly Father, as social structures and organisations seem to be crashing down, through the power of your Holy Spirit, help us to stand firm in you.

Amen

Questions for Discussion and Reflection

Before the coronavirus pandemic, what was your area of ministry or work?

Is God asking you to continue in this area of work or ministry or do you feel called to something new?

Is God asking you to slow down and take the opportunity to rest?

Is God asking you to seize a new opportunity before it passes?

Prayers

Heavenly Father, through the power of your Holy Spirit, please help us to respond wisely to the coronavirus pandemic and the current limitations of our lives. Deliver us from any spirit of fear and panic, keep us save within your strong tower.

Heavenly Father, through the power of your Holy Spirit, please show us clearly what work or ministry we should or shouldn't engage with.

Heavenly Father, please illuminate the path with the light of your precious word, protect us from becoming spiritually paralysed by fear, help us to take the next step.

Heavenly Father, please guide and strengthen those in leadership. And though the perimeters of our personal world may seem to be ever closing in, help us to be the light, help us to be a channel of your peace.

Amen

6: ARCHITECTURE

When Notre Dame Cathedral in Paris was ravaged by a massive fire, shocking images flooded the media. Photos and videos appeared everywhere; her charred skeletal frame glowed red with heat and dense smoke billowed into the Paris sky. As the 850 year old Gothic building's spire collapsed there were audible gasps from the crowd of onlookers. Though no lives were lost Youtubers made comparisons with the twin tower disaster. 500 firefighters worked to save the rest of the ancient structure. Costs to repair and restore the building will likely run into millions of pounds. An emotional French president vowed to launch an international fundraising scheme to rebuild the cathedral. One billion dollars were pledged in the first day. The sheer size of this amount, and the speed at which it was raised, sparked considerable outrage on social media. Many of the posts raised grave concerns about other causes being more deserving of these funds. Some voices were angry. Some were baffled by the idea of so much money being poured into a historical building.

Raising money to preserve constantly corroding church buildings can become really bothersome. Even faithful longstanding church members can grow tired in the face of endless fundraising. If church members are already giving regularly, direct requests for extra money in the form of a letter or email can really ruffle the feathers of the calmest, most generous of souls. I interviewed some Christians who secretly admitted that they would prefer to demolish a crumbling church building, sell off the land, donate the cash to charity and settle for the simplicity of having small groups which meet in people's homes. They were of the opinion that maintaining the building was an unacceptable drain on finances. In some cases it was believed to be poor stewardship. Some people whom I spoke to believed that meeting in homes, in a simple manner, was a model of Christianity which more closely replicated the lives of early Christians.

The lovely old Methodist Chapel, built in 1835, where my ancestors were 'hatched, matched and dispatched' eventually slipped into disrepair. At the time my Mum was the treasurer and I remember her being worried about the expensive repairs and inadequate funds. A difficult decision had to be made by those responsible. The building was demolished. The land was sold to a property developer. Two modern homes now occupy the spot. It was a sad and difficult time for the faithful congregation. Under the leadership of their Methodist Minister the handful of lifelong friends continued to meet every month in my Mum's lounge. When this eventually ended there was some private grumbling. The little group were encouraged to join another local congregation, and faithfully did so, but they continued to miss their own little chapel and the grumbling never really ended.

As the coronavirus pandemic sweeps across the globe even the opportunity to meet in the home of a friend is no longer a possibility. I find this to be one of the most difficult losses to come to terms with. Some of my most meaningful times of connection have been spent over a cup of tea in the home of a dear friend. I'm struggling to accept this loss, but I know that for now I must play it safe and be content with a video call. I thank God for video calls!

The church where my Dad was baptised and confirmed as a boy is an absolute barn of a place. A magnificent barn, yes, but it's huge. This glorious structure is currently boarded up, deemed to be unsafe for public worship and officially 'redundant'. The generous plot where it sits has many mature trees but it's becoming overgrown. It looks unloved, a monument to another era. The costs to restore it must be sky high. I watch. Knowing I am powerless.

Waiting for the day when it is no more. Stories like this are not uncommon in modern Britain.

Lovers of contemporary architecture and shiny modern buildings may not see the point of preserving a cold, cavernous, impractical, building. And yet pioneer visionaries who want to fund an independent modern building to house a 'mega church' can also become woefully unstuck. My own neighbourhood hosts a prime example of this. A huge modern building sits empty on a massive plot. From the outside this building looks to be in very good condition, but is totally unused by anyone and has been for well over a decade. Unsubstantiated rumours of impropriety and subterfuge haunt the local Christian grapevine. But even our local 'sheriff' who knows everything about everyone, can't shed much light on the mystery.

The coronavirus pandemic is raising difficult questions about the future of all our shared spaces. Libraries, community rooms, gyms, pubs and cafes are no longer in use. The enormity of such questions cannot be underestimated. More people than ever will be wrestling to find workable long term solutions, others will be operating on a day by day basis. In an unprecedented move as the government is instructing us not to meet with others the Church of England has suspended Sunday services and group activities until further notice. Toddler and Children's Groups, coffee mornings, church cafés and prayer groups have all been aborted. Suddenly there is a gaping hole in the daily lives of many people who use these services.

For some the church building itself can be a representation of something meaningful. And not just for those who count themselves as Christians. Many church buildings can be warmly regarded, even by the non-religious. An atheist friend spoke of her sincere distress when she caught sight of the roof of her local parish church ablaze. She explained that even though she didn't wish to attend a church meeting, she really valued the enduring presence of the church in her neighbourhood and wanted it to stay.

Another example: One evening I was out with a group of colleagues. We were walking through the city streets following a meal. We headed towards the train station. It was well past 10pm and some unsavoury characters were emerging from the darkness. One of my male colleagues, a sporting young man who was all of six feet two inches tall, and allegedly a firm non believer, insisted that we take the route which passed under the shadow of the church. He was stone cold sober and managed to convince seven adults that the church building itself would actually afford us iron clad protection. I'm uncertain about the theology of that idea, but he had real faith that we would be safer going that way, even though it was quite a detour!

In spite of the undeniable costs and on-going maintenance headaches surrounding both traditional and modern church buildings, we know that they are an important and unique part of our national heritage and landscape. Before the coronavirus pandemic hit the UK some of the most enterprising churches offered a safe space to meet with others. Many buildings served the communities they are part of, providing low cost spaces for community groups and their associated activities.

Among my most favourite church buildings were those which were open for seven days a week. These churches were always busy quietly getting on with the business of serving their communities and didn't really shout much about what they were up to. Given the austere times in which we live I found this to be is a wholly astonishing achievement. These buildings, and the folks who run them, somehow managed to serve their communities every single day of the week. There wasn't a day when the building wasn't open for some activity or other.

The Salvation Army had a particularly good track record of keeping their buildings open every day. They hosted all manner of lunch clubs and social groups. Many other church buildings were open and in use on several days of the week. In some cities it was possible to do a circuit of churches and get a free lunch in a warm building in the company of others on every single day of the week. This kind of organised connection just wouldn't be possible without a large building. As we enter a season when large gatherings are temporarily off limits I'm praying for the future of these treasured structures.

Questions for Discussion and Reflection

Which style of architecture do you prefer? Contemporary or Gothic?

Have you ever visited a cathedral? What was the occasion?

Are you affected by the beauty of church buildings?

How would you feel if your local church building had to be demolished?

Prayers

Heavenly Father, thank you for the rich heritage of church buildings in Britain and for all those who have worked and contributed towards maintaining and preserving them.

Heavenly Father, as the way we do church together has changed so dramatically in such a short space of time, grant us the grace to accept these new ways of being church.

Heavenly Father, as we each face an uncertain future, grant us the grace to trust steadily in you and take things one day at a time.

Heavenly Father, help us to realise that we were never in control anyway. Help us to let go of our illusions.

Amen

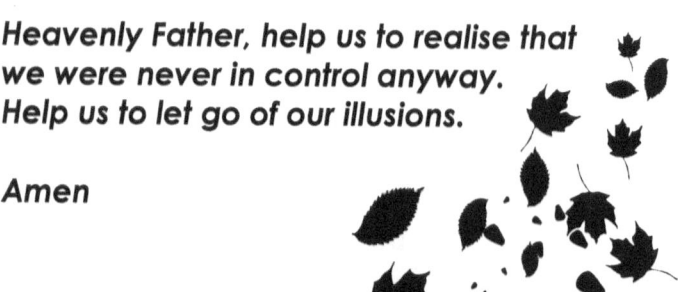

Questions for Discussion and Reflection

What spiritual resources do you already own?

Can you revisit favourite books and teachings?

How long has it been since you listened to a treasured worship album?

Have you explored Christian broadcasting such as radio, television and podcasts?

Prayers

Heavenly Father, please help us to accept that houses which were built on sand will be washed away by this storm. Please open our eyes to anything which we may have wrongly relied on for our security and salvation- our personal sand castles.

Heavenly Father, please help us to accept how precarious some things truly are, help us to come to terms with uncertainty.

Heavenly Father, please help us to rebuild our lives on solid foundations.

Heavenly Father, please help us to care for the temple where you dwell, help us to care for our own bodies, give us hope for the future.

Amen

7: ACCEPTANCE

Four whole weeks. Four whole weeks of being stuck in hospital. Confined to bed. Unable to get up and around. Having others doing everything for me. And worst of all I had to endure the heartbreak of separation from my very young children. That's the sum total of my personal experience of seriously limited living. It's not much experience to draw on really is it?

As the government guidelines about social distancing and isolation have been ramped up, so many of us, especially the do-ers, will find ourselves floundering from time to time. We've been told we must stay at home. These measures have been extreme, unprecedented. They have swept over us with all the speed and force of a tsunami. Our regular church and social activities have disintegrated as the sheer weight of this strange new reality has come crashing down with a mighty force upon our heads.

It's the most dreadful shock to the system. I find myself trying to process this new information during uninvited moments of what I can only describe as surreal day dreaming. Physically I'm on automatic pilot while brushing my teeth; mentally I'm trying to re-calibrate the new direction which a project must take. It may look as if I'm just waiting for the kettle to boil, but I'm wrestling with my ever shifting purpose for the day. Ordinary tasks like washing the dishes regularly generate inner struggles about how my loved ones will get by from day to day.

These unintentional thinking moments are like the little bubbles in a glass of fizzy water. They rise upwards at varying speeds, bumping into each other along the way. Each bubble shares the same glass and is aiming for the same destination yet they are all racing against the clock, competing for air time, in the brief window of available head space. The driving need to be heard sends them soaring towards the surface, in a bid to dissipate their charge of energy. A tiny world of concerns is packed inside in each minute sparkling globe of gas. Their eruption dances onto the boiling turbulence of the surface. Our thought life is bound to be unsettled at times. There's so much new information to process. I accept this mental state of temporary turbulence as part of the normal workings of the human mind. Each concern must rise at its own speed, each worry must be released to God. In these troubling moments be kind and accepting towards yourself, Our Heavenly Father knows what you need.

Learning how to live mostly at home is a new experience for many people. I believe that those who have been housebound for long periods of their lives are now the experts in this field. They have a wealth of knowledge about how to manage the long days and the loneliness. Existing entirely in one habitat is what they know best. They have tried and tested strategies for managing their own mental health and we could learn a lot from these quiet folks.

Of course being unwell at home and being physically fit at home are not quite the same things are they? Having lots of energy, while being confined to a small space, is more akin to a prison sentence than living with a long term disability. And so in this strange topsy-turvy world even a criminal serving a prison sentence will understand more about the realities of confined living than most of us. I have it on good authority that, in prison life, routines are a vital component for survival. One inmate told me that if you are young and physically fit it's very important to find constructive ways to burn off your surplus energy. A daily routine of regularly exercising on the spot, followed by stretching, is a good option. He also recommended, where it is safe to do so, never to forgo opportunities for daylight and fresh air. Having some shape and structure to the day was also a helpful practice to get into.

Some disabled Christian bloggers are now writing about how they live their lives indoors. Perhaps it's time to listen to these previously unheard 'little voices'. Perhaps we can benefit from the experience and wisdom they are so generously and publicly sharing. During my own time at home I've rearranged the furniture in our conservatory. I've placed two chairs and a small side table about a metre away from the door which opens onto the garden. This furniture now blocks the view from other parts of the house but I don't mind that at all. A couple of times a day I break off from my work and sit there with a cup of tea. I open the door and just watch the birds flitting about or I focus on the clouds moving slowly across the sky. Sometimes I just rest my eyes and listen to the sounds. If it's raining I still open the door for a few minutes. This practise helps to slow down my mind and I feel more connected to the natural world. The fresh air and daylight revive me.

I think of this area of the house as my personal hermitage. It's a good place to pray. Every day I give my concerns to God, I pray for others, I pray for myself. A renewed sense of gratitude for the very simplest of things often overwhelms me and I find myself dissolved in private tears while giving thanks to my Heavenly Father. I cannot overstate how wonderfully releasing this is.

Stretching my legs in the garden has brought surprising blessings. A wave to a neighbour. And unexpected early bloom. A tweet from my good friend the Robin. That well loved British pastime of visiting the garden centre may be off the agenda for the time being but that won't silence the local bird life or make the sky any less blue. In spring and summer I often do battle with some flowers which I consider as weeds. Common Dog Violets, self seeded Foxgloves, Yarrow and an invasion of Spanish bluebells are among the yearly perpetrators. This year, particularly in the absence of shop bought annuals, I'm very happy to see their accidental loveliness and will let them stay. Their resilience and perseverance have finally earned them their place and it gives me hope that these qualities can bring eventual triumph. Accepting flowers, circumstances and even people which we haven't intentionally chosen for ourselves can be a difficult, humbling but eventually liberating experience. The Dog Violets are really tenacious and used to spring up everywhere and aggravate the living daylights out of me. Now that I've made my mind up to just relax and enjoy them they seem quite sweet little things.

A pattern of opening, then later on closing windows, every day feels like therapeutic self-care. Even on a chilly day I aim to get a current of air through from the back of the house to the front for at least thirty minutes. I set the kitchen timer to remind me when the thirty minutes is up. If it's cold I just shove an extra layer on. If it's mild I leave the windows open for longer.

The headlines are pretty grim but I know that sticking my head in the sand won't be helpful for my fertile imagination. A self generated apocalypse movie storyline is not what I need right now. Keeping up with the facts about how the coronavirus pandemic is unfolding is important and helpful for me, but I know it's all too easy to overdo it and give myself a panic attack. As long as I'm following the government guidelines and doing everything I can to protect myself, the NHS and others, there's no value in scaring myself silly. It just won't help me or anyone else. Getting this balance right is a tricky exercise as the goal posts keep moving. I'm currently accessing the new updates and social media no more than twice a day (subject to on-going reviews and depending on how grumpy this makes me feel).

While I'm avoiding scaring myself silly I'm not avoiding facing my fears. In my experience, fear, much like pain, has the potential to teach us something important. Fear can generate responses similar to those generated by carbs. When I'm experiencing low level stress I crave carbs terribly and have a relentless love hate relationship with them. Consuming the right amount of good healthy carbs gives increased positive energy which carries you in the necessary direction– think Marathon runners. Consuming excessive quantities of highly processed carbs will result in energy slumps, poor sleep, a horrible twitchiness and manic cravings.

Especially among Christians fear gets a terrible press but I believe that a healthy sort of fear can be our true friend. When fear takes the shape of caution, self-preservation, risk aversion it is a sort of energy which drives us to take protective action. The whispers generated by an intuitive sense of foreboding can warn us to stay away from real danger. We ignore these whispers at our peril.

Questions for Discussion and Reflection

What's the longest period of time you've been housebound or confined to bed?

Do you have friends or relatives who have ever been confined to home, hospital or prison?

What are your current practices regarding news consumption and social media feeds?

What helps you to slow down your mind?

Prayers

Heavenly Father, thank you for places of safe shelter. Thank you for the architects, builders and workforce who have designed and built shelters for us to live in.

Heavenly Father, please help those whose shelters are not safe. Speak order into the instability and chaos of their troubled lives. By the power of your Holy Spirit help us to find ways of supporting those who are struggling to be safe.

Heavenly Father, please grant us the grace to accept these new ways of being at home. Please give us creative solutions to our daily challenges.

Heavenly Father, we are trusting you for the safety and well-being of our own lives and for those of the people we love and care about.

Amen

QUESTIONS FOR DISCUSSION AND REFLECTION

HAVE YOU ANY FEARS AND PHOBIAS?

CAN YOU RECALL A TIME WHEN GOD PROTECTED YOU FROM A SERIOUS THREAT?

DO YOU THINK GOD CAN WHISPER WARNINGS TO US?

DO YOU BELIEVE IN GUARDIAN ANGELS?

WHICH WORSHIP SONGS GIVE YOU COURAGE?

Prayers

Heavenly Father, please help us to accept the limitations of our present circumstances. Protect us from thinking of this season as 'dead' time when we're unable to make useful progress with anything.

Heavenly Father, please help and protect members of the NHS, the emergency services and the armed forces. Oh merciful God hear our cries, we need your help now more than ever.

Heavenly Father, please help us to be realistic and to accept that we are living in dangerous times. Help us to accept that the threat to health is real and we are not being silly or weak when we sometimes experience a sense of foreboding.

Heavenly Father, help us to understand that though we must hold this present reality with all seriousness in the one hand, there is no need to let fear overtake us because you are gripping our other hand and will never let us go.

Amen

8: ADAPTATIONS

Shrewd entrepreneurs have always moved in to promote and monetize commodities which people place a value on. Once upon a time football was a game which was played purely for fun. Now it is a highly profesionalized, commercialised industry. The stakes are high. It's this monetization of something which people love, for good or ill, which fundamentally changes everything. When something which is loved evolves to become an enterprise with paid staff and a profit and loss sheet, a dynamic shift occurs. The stakeholders change. The decision making power and control of funds is a magnet for the ambitious. A hierarchy may emerge. Gatekeepers are appointed. Livelihoods are influenced. On the strength of these livelihoods, and subsequent incomes, mortgages are awarded. Car loans are approved. Education is funded. Pensions are grown. Providence, security and stability are important cards on the table. There is everything to play for.

The same might be said of other 'feel good industries' such as literature, music, entertainment, tourism and yes, even faith organisations. It's so easy for us to become distracted, or wholly preoccupied, by the razamatazz surrounding some ventures. We tend not to think of faith organisations as being part of an industry, as the terms 'faith industry' and 'faith business' aren't part of our Christian vocabulary. Instead we refer to these organisations as 'ministries'. In each of these 'feel good industries' it's easy to fixate upon the lives of the players and miss the brilliance and sheer fun of the playing. It's easy to focus on the comings and goings, the job openings, the standards or lack thereof, the numbers, the profiles, the platforms. It's easy to lose sight of the inherent value.

There's an unmistakable language and culture to coastal life. And with its exhilarating air, big skies and dramatic scenery the coast has the power to lift our mood. Entrepreneurs have monopolised this 'feel good' factor. Not unlike the experience of attending church, our experience of visiting the coast, may vary enormously. Staying at a poorly equipped hotel with unhelpful staff may blight our opinion of the coast, but the coast itself will not be changed one jot by our opinions. The sea won't lose her power and the sky will not diminish. Visiting a beautifully appointed hotel with helpful, friendly staff may enhance our opinion of the coast. Nevertheless, I maintain, the coast itself will not be changed one jot by our fickle opinions. Our degree of personal comfort or discomfort won't cause the sea to increase or lessen in power or the sky to grow any larger or smaller.

And so it is with God. Our perceptions of God do not change Him or make Him any less powerful. God is exactly the same as He was before the blight of the coronavirus pandemic brutally deconstructed our daily lives. Whether we're exhibiting the symptoms of coronavirus and worshipping completely alone in the self-isolation cave of our bedroom, or in a glorious cathedral singing with a mighty throng, God has not changed. God is just as concerned for the weary soul who is desperately ill and mentally on his knees in a hospital ward as He is for all the angels of heaven. We are the ones who have changed, we are feeling different, we are out of sorts, our position seems to be shifting. But as the strange new landscape of our lives slowly emerges we must adapt and find new ways of being the church, new ways to connect with others, new patterns of spiritual practice *in the here and now*.

In a cupboard upstairs I have a long cardboard tube. Rolled up inside the cardboard tube is a poster made from an old black and white photograph. It's quite a well known photograph of a famous building. Years ago there was a short documentary on the television about the teams of people who worked in shifts to put out the fires at St Paul's Cathedral during the blitz. The grim scene of St Paul's (sometimes referred to as the Parish Church of England) standing proud among the rubble and smoke was captured for posterity in this remarkable wartime shot. The following day over a cup of tea I raved about the courageous story to my Mum and she very kindly ordered the poster as a gift for me. I feel that image is a fitting representation of an invisible threat. Now is the time for me to take that poster out of the tube. Now is the time to remind myself that the church has survived. The church, that is to say the flesh and blood church made up of flawed folks just like me and you, has been responding and adapting to crisis and drama for two thousand years. God has somehow kept his church operational right through the very worst of times and His power is not diminished by our present discomfort and troubles.

Questions for Discussion and Reflection

Can you recall any war time stories passed down through your family?

What's the worst crisis you have survived and what helped you get through it?

How important is it for you to belong to a church?

What strategies and practices could you put in place to stay connected with church friends?

Prayers

Heavenly Father, by the power of your Holy Spirit, please give us a new found appreciation for our fellow Christians, and for the wider global church of which we are a part.

Heavenly Father, please give us a new found enthusiasm to keep our church connections alive, using whatever means are currently available to us without taking any risks to health.

Heavenly Father, please give us a new found stamina and determination to repair old connections, to reach out to friends from the past, to phone them and ask after them.

Heavenly Father, please give us a new found energy to make new connections, however limited these may be. Help us to wave and smile at the neighbours from a safe distance, help us to be kind and respectful towards delivery workers, supermarket staff, and those working in the health and care services.

Amen

QUESTIONS FOR DISCUSSION AND REFLECTION

WHAT ARE YOUR PRESENT DISCOMFORTS AND TROUBLES AND HOW ARE YOU COPING WITH THEM?

WHAT ARE YOUR WORST FEARS AND HOW ARE YOU COPING WITH THEM?

DO YOU BELIEVE THE CHURCH, AS WE KNOW IT, CAN SURVIVE THE CORONAVIRUS PANDEMIC?

DO YOU THINK ANY GOOD COULD COME OUT OF THE CORONAVIRUS PANDEMIC?

Prayers

Heavenly Father, we thank you for the scientists who are advising the government. Please grant them wisdom and clarity, clearly show them the best course of action to take. Help them to navigate a way through the storm and effectively communicate their message to the masses.

Heavenly Father, we thank you for the vital infrastructures which are already in place. Thank you that we have access to clean running water, effective sanitation, food chains, a network of roads, communication channels, hospitals and emergency services. Thank you for those who will be drafted in to help us such as postal workers and the armed forces.

Heavenly Father, we thank you for your powerful hand working to preserve and protect the church in days gone by. In spite of the grim reality of our present circumstances please grow in us a new found hope in our own futures and in the future of the church.

Heavenly Father, we thank you for all those working to keep us informed and updated. Please protect those who are seeking to be tellers of the truth, the journalists, the producers and the broadcast engineers working behind the scenes.

Heavenly Father, we thank you for those who have worked to preserve and protect your precious word. Now more than ever help us to cling to your word and immerse ourselves in it. Please grow in us a new found resilience and spiritual strength. Heavenly Father help us to seek you afresh and allow you to soak our weary souls in the truth of your everlasting love.

Amen

ALSO FROM VAL FRASER

LIFE IN CARDIGANS is part memoir, part story, part rant. A rich collection of stories each inspired by at least one cardigan. From the beautiful hand-knitted creation gifted from a special auntie to the mass produced synthetic rag worn only for painting and cleaning, these touching and often funny stories, discover worth and meaning in something as ordinary as a cardigan.

THE BLESSING DIARIES

Discover the meaning of blessing in this rich collection of musings and meditations. Val Fraser has successfully gathered a creative crowd of gifted free thinkers who see the world with vibrant freshness. Together they have explored and expressed through the timeless art of poetry and story telling, reflection and striking imagery, their deeply personal understanding of the meaning of blessing.

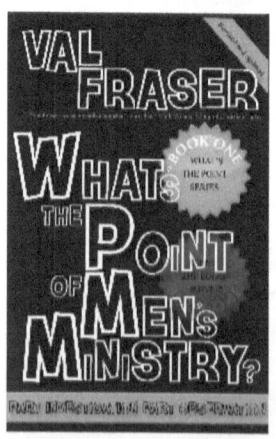

WHAT'S THE POINT OF MEN'S MINISTRY?

This title has been revised and updated and is now available in both hard copy and ebook formats.

New Life: Reflections for Lent is a collection of creative pieces published by the Association of Christian Writers. Val Fraser is one of the contributors.

BEYOND THE BANTER

Written by Bob Fraser and edited by Val Fraser, this book is a daring discussion about life and faith for blokes. The style and content make it ideal for blokes starting out on a journey of discovery, but it's equally valuable for those who've been on the road for a while and long to get stuck into the meatiness of proper conversations.

STILL CHURCH?

Can we still connect despite the coronavirus pandemic? A resource to help Christians stay connected.

ABOUT THE AUTHOR

Val Fraser is a wearer of long cardigans and a writer of short books. She has a working background in journalism and communications and was the Communications Officer for the Diocese of Liverpool before joining UCB as their Creative Writer. She has worked with the Communications Team at the Diocese of Manchester and reports for Christian Today and other news organisations.

Books from Val: *Life in Cardigans; The Case for Cardigans; The Cardigan Diet; What's The Point of Men's Ministry; Beyond the Banter* (editor); *The Blessing Diaries* (contributor/editor), *St Church*. She contributed to *New Life: Reflections for Lent* published by the Association of Christian Writers.

@ValFraserAuthor   ValFraserAuthor

www.valfraserauthor.com

ABOUT INHOUSEMEDIA

Inhousemedia is an emerging, independent micro publisher based in the northwest of England. Operationally we function as a non-profit, project-based collective. We specialize in creating original resources which are locally and lovingly produced, sympathetic to the Christian faith and mindful of ethical values.

Our products are available to buy online and at live events. Prices are kept as low as possible - all CDs are a fiver . We regularly raise funds for our favourite charities.

While our books and music CDs have faith elements within them, and are underpinned by a faith in God, we hope they are gentle enough to be valued and enjoyed by those on the fringes of faith communities and beyond.

RESOURCES FROM inhousemedia

The latest Bob Fraser audio CDs are packed with original songs. New releases, audio previews, CDs and digital downloads available at www.bob.frasermusic.com

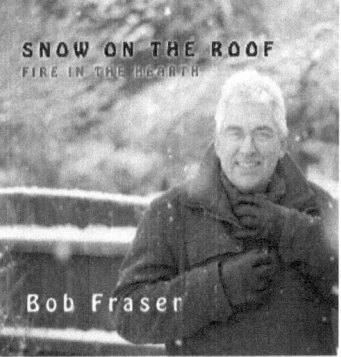

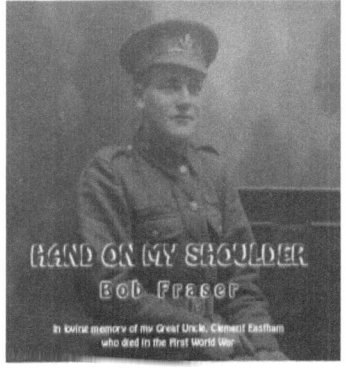

www.ingramcontent.com/pod-product-compliance
Lightning Source LLC
Chambersburg PA
CBHW030454010526
44118CB000118/930